PIANO SOLO

GAME OF THRONES™

ORIGINAL MUSIC FROM THE HBO® TELEVISION SERIES

ISBN 978-1-4950-7711-1

HAL•LEONARD®

7777 W. BLUEMOUND RD. P.O. BOX 13819 MILWAUKEE, WI 53213

In Australia Contact:
Hal Leonard Australia Pty. Ltd.
4 Lentara Court
Cheltenham, Victoria, 3192 Australia
Email: ausadmin@halleonard.com.au

Visit Hal Leonard Online at
www.halleonard.com

THE BEAR AND THE MAIDEN FAIR

By RAMIN DJAWADI
and GEORGE R.R. MARTIN

hon - ey up in her hair.
roared, and he smelled her there.

He smelled her on the sum - mer air, _____
She kicked her and wailed, the maid so fair. _____

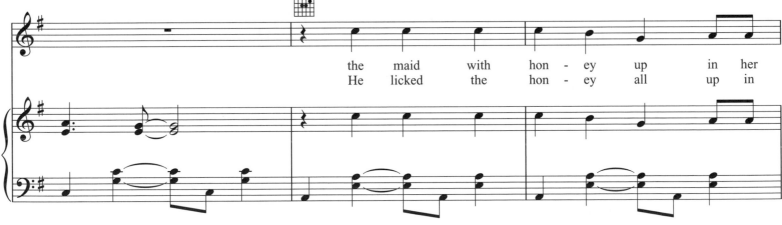

the maid with hon - ey up in her
He licked the hon - ey all up in

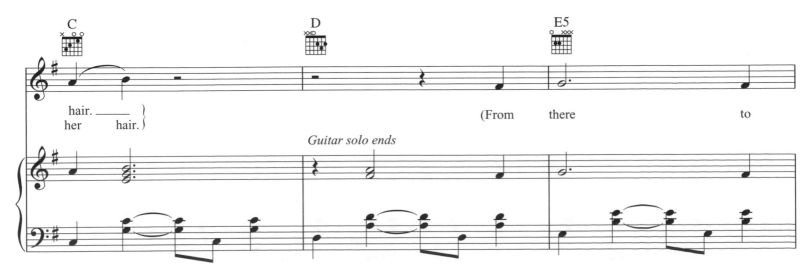

hair. _____
her hair.

(From there to

Guitar solo ends

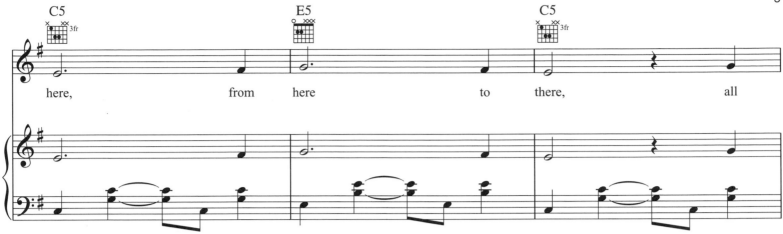

here, from here to there, all

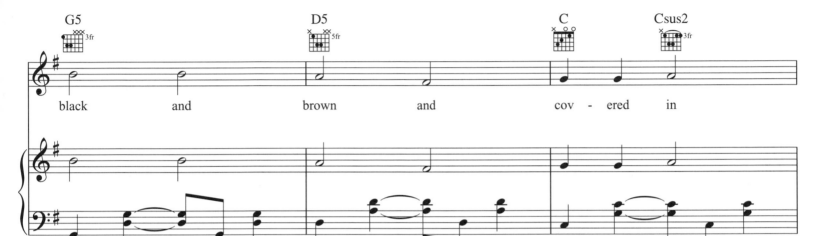

black and brown and cov - ered in

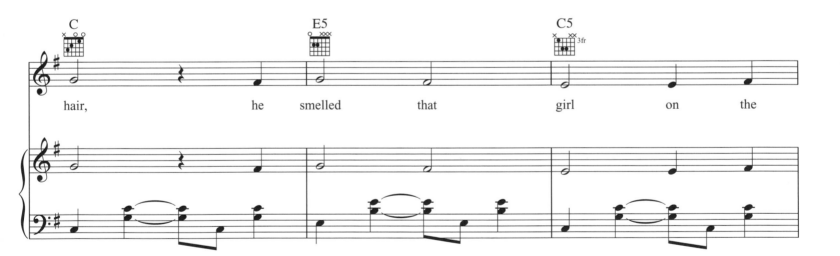

hair, he smelled that girl on the

sum - mer air. The bear, the bear,...) ...the

THE CHILDREN

By RAMIN DJAWADI

Slowly, freely

Moderately fast, steadily

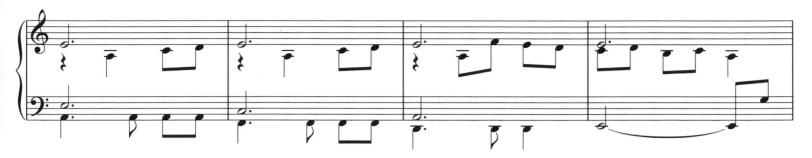

FINALE

By RAMIN DJAWADI

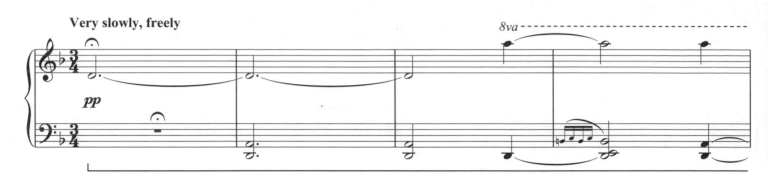

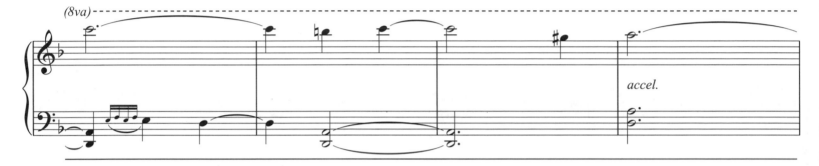

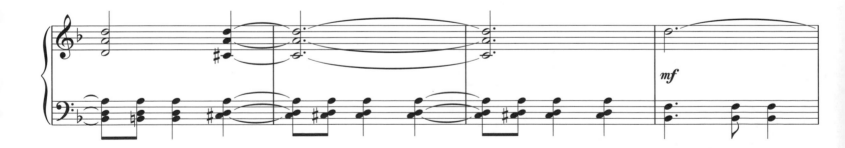

GAME OF THRONES

Music by RAMIN DJAWADI

Moderately fast

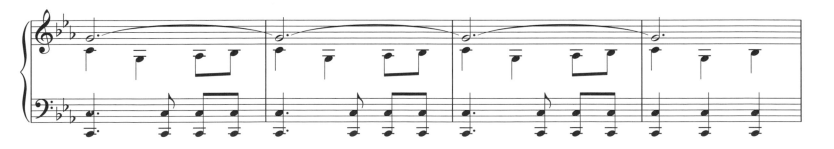

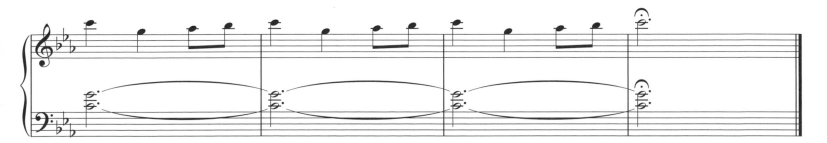

GOODBYE BROTHER

By RAMIN DJAWADI

Slowly, very freely

pp

Pedal ad lib. throughout

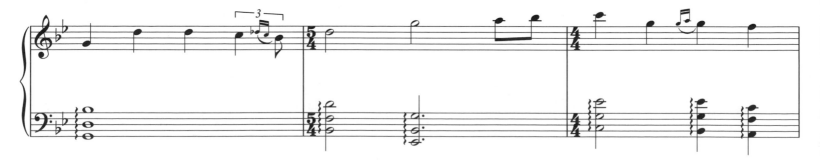

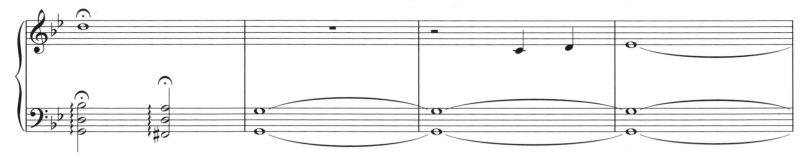

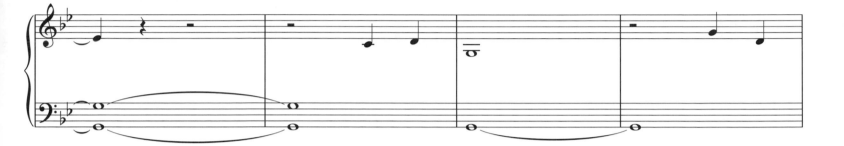

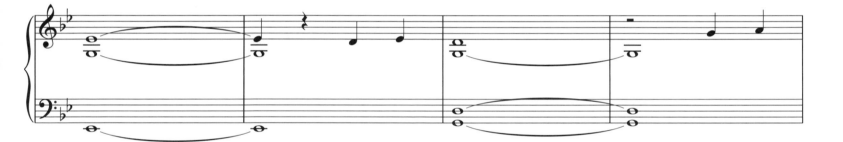

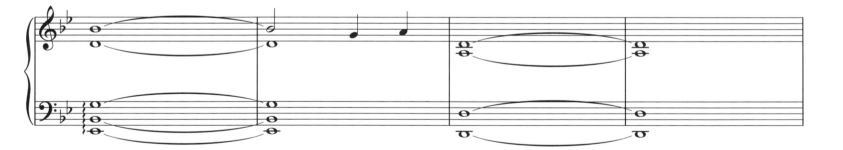

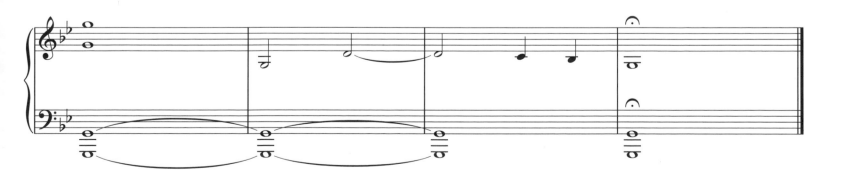

A LANNISTER ALWAYS PAYS HIS DEBTS

By RAMIN DJAWADI

molto rit.

LIGHT OF THE SEVEN

By RAMIN DJAWADI

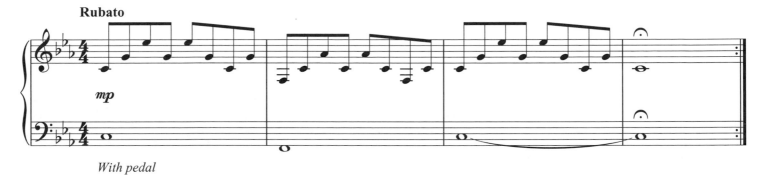

26

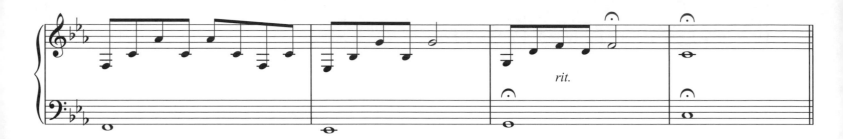

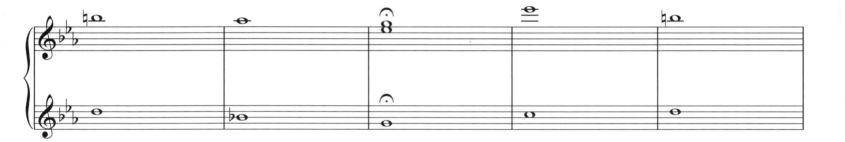

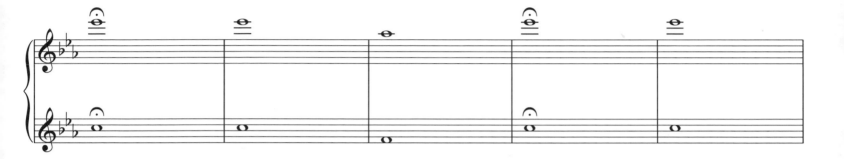

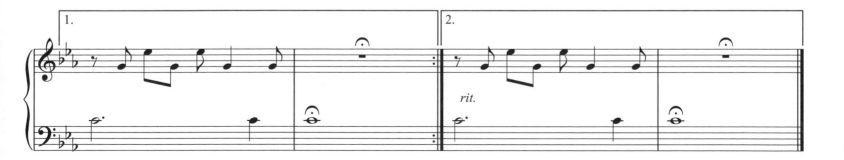

MHYSA

By RAMIN DJAWADI

Very slowly, freely

_pp_

Moderately slow, expressively

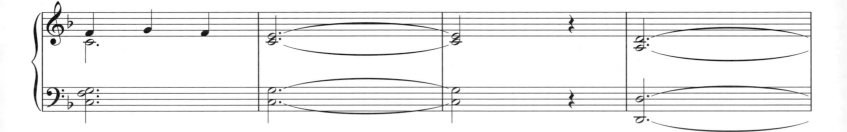

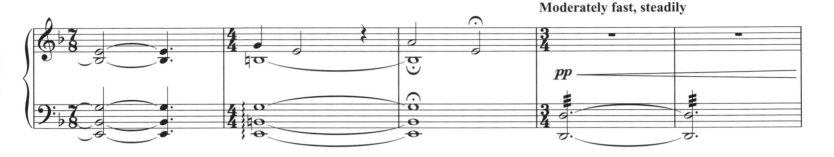

Moderately fast, steadily

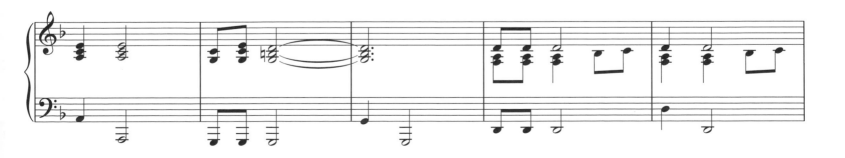

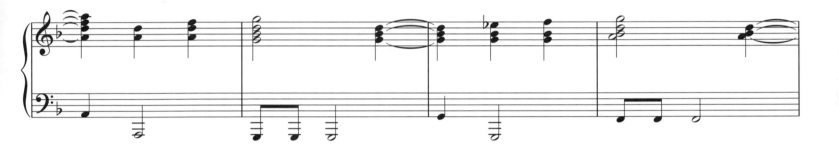

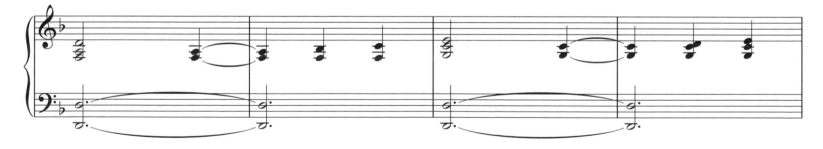

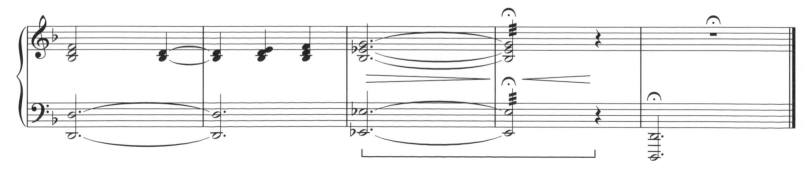

THE RAINS OF CASTAMERE

By RAMIN DJAWADI
and GEORGE R.R. MARTIN

Moderately

"All night I'll hold on you, ____ ooh, ____ you.

Cas - ta - mere, Cas - ta - mere,

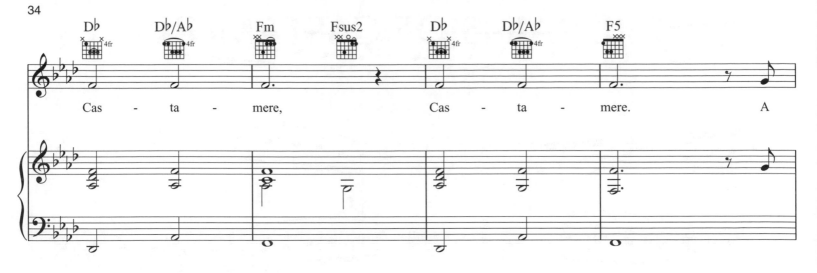

Cas - ta - mere, Cas - ta - mere. A

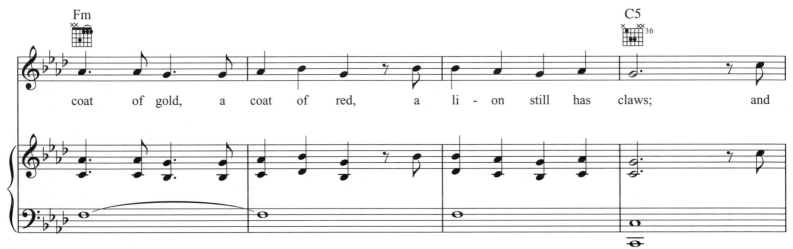

coat of gold, a coat of red, a li - on still has claws; and

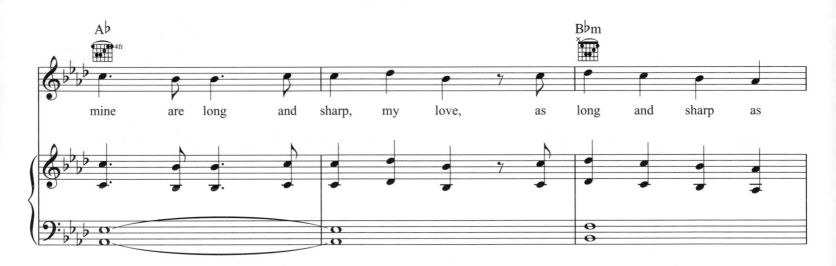

mine are long and sharp, my love, as long and sharp as

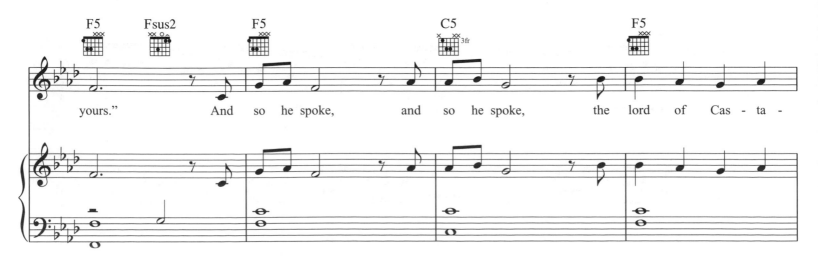

yours." And so he spoke, and so he spoke, the lord of Cas - ta -

mere.　　　　　　　　But　now　the　rains　　weep ___ o'er　his　hall　　with

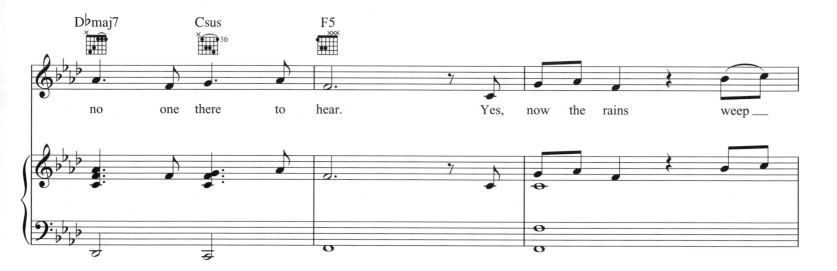

no　one　there　to　hear.　　　　　　Yes,　now　the　rains　　weep ___

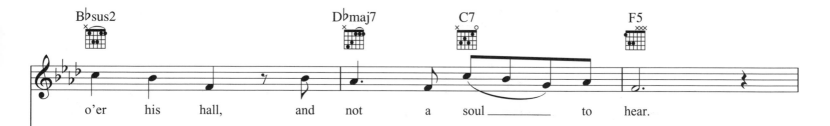

o'er　his　hall,　　and　not　a　soul _____ to　hear.

THE WINDS OF WINTER

By RAMIN DJAWADI

Moderately fast

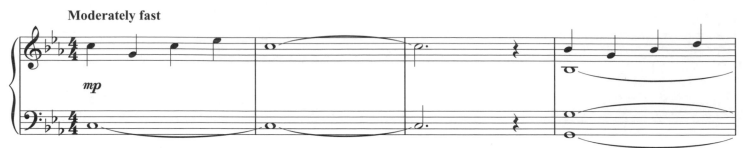

Pedal ad lib. throughout

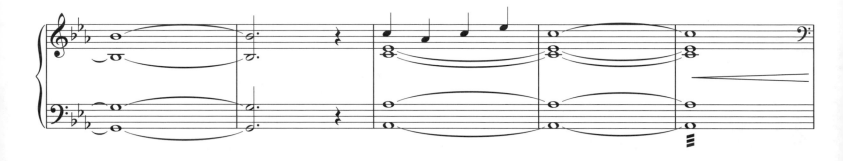

THRONE FOR THE GAME

By RAMIN DJAWADI

Slowly, freely

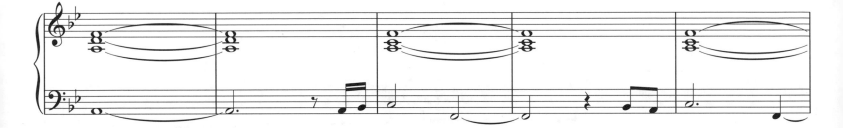

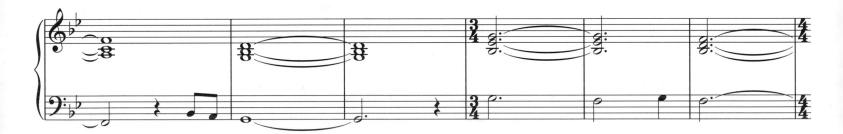